CW01221501

This book belongs to
Miss Weber

The Nature in Close-up Series
1   The Life of a Butterfly
3   Food Chains
4   The Garden Spider
5   The Dragonfly
6   Honeybees
7   Insects we Need
8   Tree in a Wood
9   Moths
10 Owls
11 Life under Stones
12 Waterside Birds
13 Frogs and Toads
14 Wasps
15 Pond Life
16 Seabirds
17 Foxes
18 Town Birds
19 Beetles
20 Snakes
21 Ants
22 Rabbits
23 Mice
24 Badgers

> Clay, Pat and Helen
> Pond life.—(Nature in close-up; 15)
> 1. Pond flora—Great Britain—Juvenile literature
> 2. Pond fauna—Great Britain—Juvenile literature
> I Title   II. Clay, Helen   III. Series
> 587.941   QH137
> ISBN 0-7136-2212-1

Published by A & C Black (Publishers) Limited
35 Bedford Row, London WC1R 4JH

First published 1982
Reprinted 1984

© 1982 Pat and Helen Clay

All rights reserved. No part of this publication may be reproduced, stored in a retrieval system, or transmitted, in any form or by any means, electronic, mechanical, photocopying, recording or otherwise, without the prior permission in writing of A & C Black (Publishers) Limited

Filmset by August Filmsetting, Haydock, Merseyside
Printed in Hong Kong by Dai Nippon Printing Company

Nature in Close-up

POND LIFE

Pat and Helen Clay

Adam and Charles Black · London

Contents

Introduction 3
Ponds 4
Pond dipping 6
Animals on the surface of the pond 8
Animals near the top of the pond 10
Animals that dive 13
Underwater nurseries 15
Animals that breathe underwater 18
Animals that live in the mud 20
The balance of nature 24
Index 25

Introduction

Where do you think you would find this frightening looking creature? In a dark cave? At the bottom of the sea? In fact, it is only 30 mm long and you would find it in a pond.

The Great Diving Beetle is one of the fiercest creatures in a pond. It eats many small animals and will even attack fish or frogs. Most of the time, it lives underwater. But in the evenings, you can sometimes see it flying from pond to pond.

This book looks at some of the animals in a pond and tells you how they live. It also shows where you might find them. But remember that most of these animals can move around, so you might not always find them where you expect to.

◀ Great diving beetle

▲ Overshadowed pond

Ponds

There are three main kinds of pond.
Overshadowed ponds have trees and bushes growing over them. The water is clogged up with fallen leaves. These ponds don't get much sunshine, so not many plants or animals can live in them.

Open Ponds are warmed by the sun and attract many different kinds of birds and animals. The plants which grow in these ponds provide food and oxygen for all sorts of water creatures.

Temporary Ponds are shallow patches of water. They freeze in the winter and dry up in the summer. Frogs, toads, newts and the larvae of some water beetles live in these ponds. They can only survive because they spend part of their lives on land.

Sunlight is very important to the animals and plants which live in ponds. Other things, such as the time of year, the weather and the soil around the pond can also affect pond life.

▲ Open pond   ▼ Temporary pond

Pond dipping

One of the best ways to find out about water creatures is to go pond dipping.

Here are some of the things you might need.
1 A sieve that has a strong handle, so you can drag it through the mud (a metal flour sieve is ideal).
2 A net which is fine enough to catch even the smallest animals (nylon nets are the strongest).
3 A white tray, or dish, to tip the creatures into, so you can see them.
4 A magnifying glass to examine the animals.
5 A jar to carry home anything for further study.
6 A notebook and pencil.

Before you start pond dipping, write down the date, place and what kind of pond you are studying. Then, sit quietly by the side of the pond. You might see some of the land creatures which are attracted to the water; birds, small mammals or even a grass snake taking a swim.

You might hear the 'plop' of a frog landing in the pond, or see frogs' spawn floating on the water. In spring, tadpoles hatch out of the spawn. They are a very important kind of food for many of the animals in the pond.

Common frog ▶

Animals on the surface of the pond

Some insects can run over the surface of the pond without sinking. You can catch them by skimming your net over the top of the water.

Pond Skater

The pond skater has hairs on its legs and under its body. These hairs stop the animal from getting wet as it runs across the water. It has a pair of sharp claws on each of its front legs. They are used to snap up small water creatures for food. Pond skaters can fly. During the winter, they hibernate on land.

▼ Pond skater

Raft Spider

Raft spiders live on the surface of ponds, but sometimes you can see them dive under the water. The female lays over 500 eggs in a silk cocoon. A few weeks later, she attaches the bundle of eggs to a plant at the edge of the pond. Then she spins a 'tent' over the top of the eggs to protect them. The young spiders hatch out in two to three weeks.

Whirlygig Beetle

These shiny blue-black beetles spend most of the day spinning round in circles on the surface of the pond. But if they are disturbed, they dive under the water. They can also squirt a horrible smelly liquid at their enemies. Whirlygig beetles feed on small insects which have fallen into the water.

▲ A water boatman, just under the surface of the pond

Animals near the top of the pond

Many pond creatures stay near the top of the pond because they have to breathe air. You might catch some of them by skimming your net just below the surface of the water.

Water Boatman

This insect is sometimes called the 'Back Swimmer' because it swims upside down. It moves through the water by using its back legs like a pair of oars. The water boatman eats insects and tadpoles. It has a sharp beak and could give you a painful bite.

Water Scorpion

Water scorpions are not very strong swimmers. They spend most of the time crawling among the plants near the top of the pond. They get the name scorpion from their long tail, which some people think is a sting. In fact, it is a breathing tube which the insect pushes above the water to get air.

Mosquito Larva

These strange creatures are the larvae, or young, of mosquitoes. The female mosquito lays her eggs in calm water. A pond or even a puddle will do. Soon, larvae emerge from the eggs. The larvae hang just below the surface of the pond. They stick their tails up above the water. These tails are hollow, so the larvae can breathe through them.

▲ A water scorpion using its breathing tube

▼ A mosquito pupa and a mosquito larva

▲ Adult mosquito

After about a week, the larva changes into a pupa. Its head becomes very large and it curls its body round into the shape of a comma. A few days later, the pupa turns into an adult mosquito.

Adult mosquitoes feed on nectar from flowers. But sometimes the female mosquito becomes a bloodsucker. Her mouth is shaped like a sharp needle, so she can pierce the skin of birds and animals. Some kinds of mosquito spread diseases such as malaria and yellow fever.

Animals that dive

Some of the animals in a pond carry their own air supply with them. This means they can stay underwater for quite a long time. You might be able to catch them as they come up for air.

Screech Beetle

The screech beetle swims to the top of the pond and traps air underneath its hard wing cases. Then, it dives down to the bottom, carrying a bubble of air. It can stay underwater as long as this air supply lasts. If you pick up a screech beetle, it will make a squeaking noise. It does this by rubbing the end of its body against the inside of its wing cases.

▼ A screech beetle with a bubble of air

▲ Saucer bug

Saucer Bug

The saucer bug carries its own air supply in the same way as the screech beetle does. It spends most of its time on the bottom of the pond, looking for food. Although it is small, it is very fierce and could bite you.

Saucer bugs can't fly. They have to crawl across land to reach other ponds. During the winter, they hibernate in the mud at the bottom of ponds.

Underwater nurseries

Pond animals need a safe place to lay their eggs. Some creatures attach their eggs to the stems or leaves of underwater plants. If you look carefully at the plants in a pond, you might see some of these eggs.

Great Pond Snail

This snail lays its eggs inside a transparent bag. The bag is stuck underneath the leaves of water plants, so the eggs can't float away.

Another common snail is the Ramshorn. It eats the green slime, called algae, which grows on water plants.

On a sunny day, you might see these snails crowding round the edges of a pond.

▲ The egg pod and young of a great pond snail

▼ Ramshorn snail

Newts

The female Common Newt lays her eggs on the leaves or stems of underwater plants.

Soon, a larva emerges from each egg. It can breathe underwater through feathery gills on each side of its head. The larva eats tiny water fleas and tubifex worms.

▼ Eggs of the common newt

As the young newt gets bigger, it develops lungs instead of gills. When it is ready, it leaves the water to live on land for two or three years.
At the end of this time, it goes back to the water to find a mate.

▲ Common newt larva   ▼ Adult common newt

Three different kinds of newt live in Britain, the Palmate Newt, the Great Crested Newt and the Common Newt, often called the Smooth Newt. They are all very shy of humans but you might find them under stones or rocks at the edges of ponds.

▲ Male stickleback

Animals that breathe underwater

If you sweep your net through the deep water of the pond, you might catch some of the creatures which can breathe underwater.

Stickleback

Sticklebacks are eaten by many of the larger fish in ponds, such as Rudd or Carp. They are also hunted by water birds and small mammals.

In spring, the male stickleback is easy to spot. The underneath of his body turns bright red. He uses his bright colours to attract a female. Then he builds a nest for the female to lay her eggs in. He will fight any enemies that try to come near the nest.

Mayfly Nymph

You can recognise the nymph, or young, of the mayfly by its long slender tails. It lives in deep water for two or three years, feeding on underwater plants.

A mayfly nymph underwater ▶

When the nymph is ready to turn into an adult, it swims to the surface of the pond and sheds its skin. It is now ready to fly, but it will shed one more skin before it becomes an adult.

Adult mayflies only live for a few hours or days. When they have mated and laid their eggs, they die.

◀ Adult mayfly

▲ Tubifex worms

Animals that live in the mud

Some very strange animals live in the mud at the bottom of ponds. If you drag your scoop through the mud, you might be able to catch them.

Tubifex Worms

Tubifex worms usually live in overshadowed or polluted ponds. Large colonies of them live upside down in little mud tubes. They feed on the bacteria of decaying leaves. These worms grow to about 8cm long and are a very important kind of food for many pond animals.

Caddis Fly Larva

The larva of the caddis fly defends itself from enemies by building a movable home. First, the larva spins a loose silk coat around its body. Then, it sticks small bits of leaf, sand, twigs or gravel onto the silk. Gradually, the larva builds a hard case around itself. It has two strong hooks on the end of its body, so it can drag the case around with it as it feeds.

When the larva is ready to turn into an adult, it bites its way out of the case and swims to the surface. The adult caddis fly looks rather like a small moth and usually flies at night.

▲ A caddis fly larva in its protective case

Adult caddis fly ▶

Damselfly

Damselflies are the smallest members of the dragonfly family. Their nymphs, or young, live at the bottom of ponds. These nymphs are fierce hunters and eat many different kinds of tiny water creatures.

▲ Damselfly nymph

When it is time for the nymph to turn into a damselfly, it pulls itself up the stem of a strong water plant. It rests above the water for a while. Then its body begins to swell. Finally, its old skin splits open and the young damselfly crawls out.

▲ A large red damselfly coming out of its old skin

Its wings are very small and crumpled at first, but they gradually become bigger and stronger. After two hours the adult damselfly is ready to fly for the first time. From then on, it lives near the pond, feeding on small gnats and flies. Its main enemies are birds, larger dragonflies and spiders.

A large red damselfly about to ▶ make its first flight

The balance of nature

A food chain

The animals and plants in a pond depend on each other for food. Each one is part of a food chain, so even the smallest animals and plants are important. For example, if there was no algae in a pond, many of the animals might die. There would not be enough food for them.

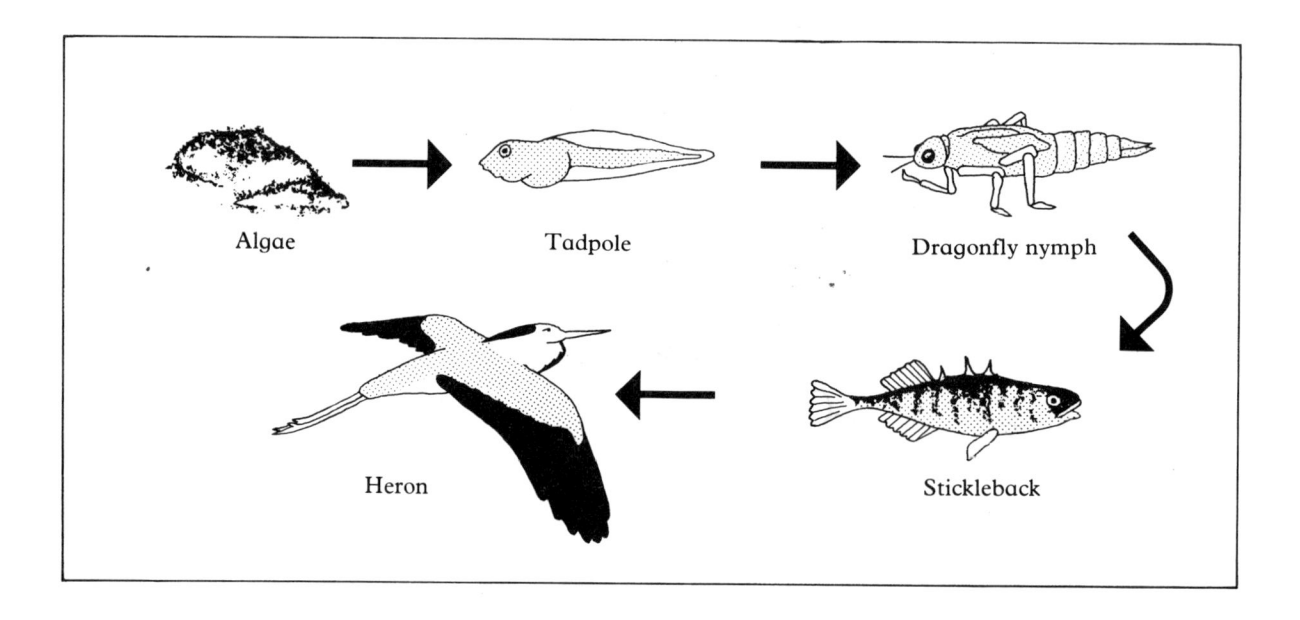

▲ A food chain. The arrows show that an animal is eaten by another. For example, algae is eaten by tadpoles

If you go pond dipping, try not to upset the balance of nature.
1 Don't take too many samples from the pond and always put back the ones you don't need.
2 If you lift up a stone, put it back gently.
3 Don't trample down the plants around the pond.
4 Take care when handling delicate water life.
5 Be as quiet as possible so you won't disturb the animals which live near the pond.
6 Take all your litter home with you.